Kintsugi

Tvisha

GRIFFIN
publication

GRIFFIN PUBLICATION

Registration No: UDYAM-UP-56-0004439
Yashoda Kunj, Mawana Road, Meerut, 205001
First Published by GRIFFIN publication 2025

ISBN: 978-93-91813-61-1
Price: 349/-

For Ma,

No number of words could possibly encompass how much I love you. Without you, there would be no me, no book, no Zoe.

Author's Note

Dear Reader,

Kintsugi (金継ぎ) - The Japanese art of repairing or restoring broken glass or pottery with gold, silver or platinum.

If only Kintsugi could be used to repair broken smiles, broken spirits, and broken souls. If only gold, silver, or platinum could fill the cracks and fix the wounds. If only Kintsugi could heal the broken, then maybe my tears wouldn't fill the sea.

I am not glass, neither am I healed. I'm not going to say that I'm okay, because I'm not. But then again, who is? And that's OK. It's OK to not be perfect. It's OK to not be OK. And it's perfectly OK to be human.

So, this is my story - told through verse. The story of pain, betrayal, and insecurities. Of finding beauty in a thunderstorm. Of coming to the realization that the dark is hauntingly scary, but it's beautiful. Infinitely more than day. That summer is pretty, but nearly not as angelic and sublime as the winter. The realization that maybe, just maybe, it's better this way. Because, what is day without night?

What is joy without sorrow?

And what is love without pain?

So, my dear reader, cry if you want to. Laugh if you want to. Scream if you want to. Do not ever care about what they say. And if they leave, they were never yours to begin with.

Now, I will conclude this freakishly and uncharacteristically mature monologue by suggesting that you enjoy this collection. And I will say just one last thing: When life gives you lemons, do not make lemonade. That is so basic! Be unique. Be different. BE YOU. And bake the most exquisite lemon meringue pie!

Love, T.

Lost & Found

"If you stare into the abyss long enough, you will notice that it will begin to stare back into you"

Friedrich Nietzsche

Dear Reader,

Have you ever felt so lost that everything feels like a fleeting dream? So lost, that your life suddenly feels like a work of your imagination? So lost, that you're just numb. You aren't happy, you aren't wallowing in your sorrow, you aren't feeling anything. And yet, somehow you are feeling everything. It's weird because you're trapped in your own cocoon and you're not able to break it open.

Friedrich Nietzsche once said "if you stare into the abyss long enough, you'll begin to notice, that the abyss begins to stare back into you". And every day, I come to the realization that he was spot on. The more you're lost, the more that sensation of being lost consumes you. It swallows your body whole, until you have not a clue of who you are anymore.

It aches. Your metamorphosis just doesn't seem to be happening any time soon. It's your world that you're trapped in. It's your world that you're lost in, and only in your world shall you be found.

Love, T.

ABSTRACT

it's scary - after all what is a lie?
Isn't the truth nothing but a why?
Who defines what is right?
Is the sun setting the same as being out of sight?
What is love? what is hate?
Why is He the architect? is it really fate?
Sometimes I feel like I am abstract art
What can I say? I'm just pretty from afar
And I don't know why, the mess, it bothers me
Inside I am but tangled yarn, the chaos, the ugly
And it hurts, the fact that I am no longer me
And the idea of being imperfect, of not being pretty...

PARADOX

It's day and night
It's wrong and right
It's yes and no
It's stop and go
It's love and hate
It's choice and fate
It's up and down
It's a smile and a frown
It's sad and yet happy
It's land but also sea
It's silence and it's noise
It's sudden and still has poise
It's a mystery waiting to unfold
It's a story waiting to be told
It has a purpose as clear as the sky
When accomplished, it's ready to die
Relations, possessions; then why does it feel incomplete?
But in pure nothingness, life seems complete?
It has magic hidden in every atom
It's a rollercoaster ride, and yet life is wholesome.

-December 3, 2021 (11 years old)

LOST

In the labyrinth of my mind, I roam,
Like a leaf in the wind, I'm aimless, alone.
Every path I take leads to a dead end,
Is it real or is it just pretend?

I'm a puzzle with missing pieces, incomplete,
Trying to find myself in a crowd on the street.
Like a ghost in the mist, I fade away,
Lost in nothingness, no light, no day.

Lost in translation, misunderstood,
In a sea of voices, I drown, I'm no good.
Like a song without rhythm, a dance without beat,
I'm wandering aimlessly with no retreat.

Lost in the noise of life's constant din,
Searching for solace, where do I begin?
Like a message in a bottle, tossed out to sea,
I'm lost in this world with no guarantee.

In the labyrinth of my mind, I roam,
But finding my way seems impossible, i'm alone.
Lost in the shuffle, a mere afterthought,
In a world so vast, where dreams come to naught.

MIRAGE

I swam in the deep, my feet couldn't touch the ground
Lost in the unknown, but myself, I found
Yet in shallow waters, I sank
Confusion, frustration, blank
In waters shallow, my senses deceived
When certainty crumbled, I grieved
Known, unknown, all blurred and swayed
For in the mirage, and clarity seemed to fade
But in the deep, I found solace profound
Where truth whispered, a tranquil sound
In the depths of the sea, my truth unveiled
Under the waves, the truth prevailed

TWO WORLDS APART

In two worlds, we dwell, you and I,
Different paths, beneath the same sky.
Once entwined, now torn apart,
Two souls adrift, with shattered hearts.

Once upon a time, our hearts beat as one,
But now our paths diverge, our connection undone.
You walk your path, I tread mine,
In separate worlds, we both resign.

Two worlds apart, but once so near,
Now distant echoes, we strain to hear.
The bond we shared, now lost to time,
Now all that's left is a rhyme.

When you say you love me

"You say you love the rain, yet you use an umbrella to walk under it.

You say you love the sun, yet you seek shade when it's shining. You say you love wind, but when it comes you shut your windows.

So, that's why I'm scared when you say you love me."

Sir William Shakespeare

Dear Reader,

Love is an enigma—intangible and undefinable, yet undeniably real. It's perplexing and strange, a mystery I can't fully grasp. Things I claim to love – books, coffee, music – feel transient, like I could stop loving them at any moment. But here, I'm not talking about materialistic love or the love one might feel for something or someone real. This is an abstract kind of love – love for an idea, an emotion, a feeling. About love.

Love is unique. Like a chameleon, it changes colour for each individual. Love isn't something you seek or acquire. Love is there in you, quietly waiting to be recognized. It's not about possession or attachment but about resonance—an alignment with something beyond yourself that makes you feel alive, whole, and connected.

But dear reader, love is paradox - beauty and pain delicately intertwined. It has the power of upliftment and inspiration just like a moth drawn irresistibly to a flame. Yet, just like that light, it might guide, or it could scorch and leave a mark on your soul.

Love, T.

A WILTED ROSE

In a garden once, a rose did dwell,
Its petals, once vibrant, now languidly fell.
Withered, forlorn, in a world of decay,
Its essence fading, hues turning grey.

Once kissed by sunlight, now shunned by shade,
Each drooping petal, a sorrow displayed.
No longer basking in the morning's glow,
But shrouded in shadows, lost in woe.

The vibrant fragrance, a memory now past,
Replaced by a scent of melancholy amassed.
Where once bees danced in joyful delight,
Now silence reigns, veiled in the night.

The stem, once proud, now bends with despair,
Its thorns dulled, stripped of their flair.
Like a forgotten dream, it lies in repose,
Petals droop in the memory of the love that once was...

ALREADY BROKEN

you showed me my flaws, all that I obsess about
what does it matter if I'm fat or thin?
is me putting on a little weight really a sin?
when I was clueless, powerless, hopeless, you sucked me in.

you can't break what's already been broken,
you can't take what's already been stolen,
you can't hate a heart already frozen,
you can't turn back time to when I was 11.

It's too late to regret,
there's too much to forget,
it pains too much, but now I don't care

I'm not going back, I've cut my hair
I'm too tired for all that I used to bear
too hurt to hide these scars on my soul that I wear
so just walk away, if you care

I was just a kid, desperate for love,
I was just a kid, who was never good enough,
I'm just a kid, who's had it way too tough,
I'm just a kid, tied up, in handcuffs.

FOR YOU

For you, I'd chase shooting stars,
And stitch together broken scars.
For you, I'd dance in the rain,
I'd wash away all the pain.

For you, I'd paint the skies anew,
In hues of red, in shades of blue.
For you, I'd sculpt the perfect dream,
Where nothing's quite as it may seem.

For you, I'd sail through stormy seas,
Pretend it was nothing, call it a gentle breeze.
For you, I'd give up all that I've ever loved and known
I'd stitch back up a heart long torn.

"For you", I've said, but who is that you?
Are they right, would I really know what to do?
They all seem to think that I don't know how to feel
That I haven't got a heart that beats, but one of steel

Are they right, are they wrong?
Would I run, or write a song?
"For you" I'd question, ponder why
For you would I live or for you would I die?

THE IDEA OF AN 'US'

when i was 13, my grandma told me a story
she told me life without love is incomplete
when i was 13, and i lost all reason to believe
because all i knew was that they would leave, she told me

"Baby, have some faith
there's someone out there for you
and just like i got my one
someday you will too
and when you do...

you'll see flowers everywhere
want to put ribbons in your hair
and smile with no reason to
your grandpa and i, we had a beautiful life
because we loved each other from our eyes
and we didn't fall in love, we walked into it
it was all so beautiful, so innocent
and someday i want that for you"

it scares me, the idea of being a we
being the other half to somebody
because what if i lose me?
and it scares me

so my grandma told me a story
about love in all its glory
and she said...
"it's beautiful to wake up next to somebody
to not live life in total monotony
to seal every day with a kiss
to always have somebody to miss
and when you find that someone...

you'll see flowers everywhere
want to put ribbons in your hair
and smile with no reason to
your grandpa and i, we had a beautiful life
because we loved each other from our eyes
and we didn't fall in love, we walked into it
it was all so beautiful, so innocent
and someday i want that for you"

and she said...
"Take a chance
don't cry in the rain, just dance
it's supposed to be beautiful
it's supposed to be a trance"

and when i was 13, my grandma told me a story
a cliché romance, with roses and tea
about the greatest man you'll ever see
about everything that i just don't believe
about everything that love is supposed to be.

WHAT I'D DO FOR YOU

I'm done for, but it's true
For you I'd turn my grey skies blue
I'd chase the stars and hope
I'd crawl up a downward slope
I'd run behind dreams I've long lost
I'd melt away my heart of ice and frost

For you I'd be the hero who saves the world,
Not the villain who burns it way
I'd turn an endless night to day
I'd trade my black boots for white stilettos
I'd make a friend of all my foes

For you I'd hug them just for them to stab me in the back
I'd fill up all the spaces and all that I lack
For you I'd give up everything
For you I'd stop the world from ending

For you I'd be everything
But to you, I apologize, for I am nothing.

A sail in the wind

"Hope is the thing with feathers that perches in the soul-and sings the tunes without the words-and never stops at all"

Emily Dickinson

Dear Reader,

It is the whispered bard that breaks the silence of a dark night. That one ray of light which refuses to dim. That one flame that cannot be snuffed out. It is the strength in your bones that keeps you trudging even when the weight of the world seems to tear you apart, reminding you that something brighter lies beyond even at your most desperate hour. It is not blind optimism; rather it is an ingrained faith in your own capability to confront the demons and rise above it towards a brighter future. It is the thread that binds you to your dreams, weaving resilience into your spirits, and painting possibilities where there once were none.

That is hope.

Hope was something I struggled to find during a rather tempestuous time in my life. I didn't have plenty of it, but the little I had, was enough to get by.

So dear reader, have hope, even if it is just a molecule of it.

Love, T.

COFFEE, THE OCEAN & SEPTEMBER DREAMS

I sit and I ponder, lost in thought

In the early light of dawn where dreams are caught

The ocean's distant roar, a soothing melody

As I drift away on the waves of possibility

Dreams dance, a kaleidoscope of hues

Whispering secrets of destiny, chasing away all blues

The salty seas carry echoes of forgotten tales

Choices seem like a flip of a coin, heads or tails?

There's just so much that I've dreamt of, so much that I want to do

Have the courage to paint the sky pink, violet or blue...

EUNOIA [yoo-noy-uh]

Another sunrise that paints the sky in hues of gold
Another sunset that brings with it stories untold
Once again, the curtain falls and the day fades away
Another night sky, the ocean waves, and first light of day

Another flower, to put in my hair
The scent of frangipanis that fill the air
Another leaf just wandering with no destination
Another thought that makes me smile, from my imagination

The scent of the earth after fresh rain
There's so much to live for, to see again
It's these beautiful thoughts that keep away the strife
It's these beautiful thoughts that make a beautiful life...

NOT TODAY

Not today, your English assignment's still not done
Not today, the weekend plans can't be overrun
Not today, that pizza place you've been eyeing
Not today, the latest Netflix series worth trying
Not today, there's another sunset to see
Not today, the world might just let you be
Not today, the moon shines bright in the sky
Not today, don't let your dreams pass by
Not today, that show's finale awaits
Not today, the excitement, the thrills, the dates
Not today, your favourite band's new hit
Not today, don't throw it away bit by bit
Not today, the thought of quitting can't win
Not today, let perseverance begin
Not today, the taste of success is near
Not today, push away every fear
Not today, the flowers bloom with grace
Not today, feel the wind kiss your face
Not today, the stars still dance in the night
Not today, you'll find reasons to fight
Not today, for the sunrise tomorrow
Not today, let go of every sorrow

Not today, there's music to discover
Not today, there's so much to uncover
Not today, the possibilities are vast
Not today, your story's not in the past
Not today, for the laughter yet to come
Not today, embrace the rhythm, the drum
Not today, the journey is worth the ride
Not today, let hope be your guide
Not today, for the taste of chocolate cake
Not today, for every move you make
Not today, for the smell of fresh-cut grass
Not today, for the moments that pass
Not today, there's so much left to see
Not today, for once listen to me
Not today, there's still a sunset to admire
Not today, there's more of life to desire
Not today, don't you dare say goodbye
Not today, let's give it another try
Not today, your English assignment's still not done
Not today, but soon it will be, and then you'll have won

REVERIE

Underneath a tree, with a canopy wide
In a world where dreams don't need to hide
Lost in a reverie's grace
Where fantasies seem to dance in this magical place

Warm raindrops fall, my face they caress
In the midst of winter, elegance and finesse
Yet in the air, there's a warmth so sweet
Where the cold and cozy finally meet

I close my eyes, put a ceasefire to the fight
In my daydream, where it all feels right
Where my dreams paint themselves in colours so bright
As reality fades into the night

Underneath the tree, I let my dreams unfurl
In my daydream, where I'm the pearl
A raindrop's kiss, washes away the blue
My daydream is an enchantment, where my dreams come true.

SUNRISE

Analogies that cause pain
Words throwing all effort in vain
Every step of this excruciating run
Is a step closer to the ebbing sun
Joy, ecstasy, is it all pretend?
Hurt, pain, does it ever end?
Why does the sun seem to fade so soon?
Why am I blinded to the rising moon?
A myriad of afflictions, why on my road?
Why is it that I write this ode?
That sings the tune of a devoid in a heart
Thoughts turned obscure from the start
A fear of oblivion makes its way
Fear takes over, says what it has to say
Expectations unsatisfied, a fear of imperfection
Agony, anguish, a changed expression
The time has now come, the sun out of sight
While the sun is gone, the moon shines its light
But what most, choose to forget
Is that the sun rises, after it has set

(12.12.2022, 12 years old)

SUNSET

when the sun decides to retire for the day
painting the skies in hues of gold and grey
the world holds its breath, in silent awe
as the sun bids adieu with a lethargic drawl,
the horizon becomes a canvas, ablaze
with fiery strokes in its final phase
but honey, don't let the dusk bring you down
for when the sun sets, it casts a ray of gold upon our little town
and as the sun dips low, and kisses the earth
you truly realize its beauty and worth
but it's okay, because the moon will rise, our silver queen
reflecting the sun's light onto all of the unseen
so, as the sun fades out of view
remember the night has its own debut
for in the darkness, secrets lie
underneath the vast, starry sky
so, love, and cherish the sun but also embrace the night
because the both are beautiful, unique and one of a kind.

Academic Validation is Toxic? Who would've Known...

"Some are born great, some achieve greatness, some have greatness thrusted upon them."

Sir William Shakespear

Dear Reader,

Academic validation. Who needs self-worth, intrinsic motivation, or personal growth when you can just collect gold stars on your report card? After all, nothing screams "I've made it in life" quite like a high GPA and a few certificates hanging on your wall. Forget about cultivating meaningful relationships or developing a sense of purpose; if you're not getting straight A's, what's the point of even trying?

Isn't it just delightful how the world equates your entire value as a human being to how well you can regurgitate information onto a test paper? It's almost poetic, really. The thrill of being praised for memorizing facts you'll forget the moment the exam ends is nothing short of exhilarating. Who wouldn't want to spend their formative years chasing after the next big academic achievement like a hamster on a wheel? The harder you run, the more you get to prove you're the best-trained rodent in the cage.

So dear reader, I've sought enough approval to know that you must chase your dreams, not validation. Your worth isn't determined by a report card or anyone else's opinion. Do not let anyone or even a measly piece of paper define who you are. You and only you have the right to decide who you are and who you aspire to be.

Love, T.

LITTLE MISS PERFECT

Everyone adored her
she made it look like a breeze
her fingers danced across the keys
until they fell off

all I did was work
but a I tried to be happy
to him I was everything that he couldn't be
but I quit

the perfect grades
the perfect smile
no one knew that she wanted to die inside
but the wind got too strong
the perfection felt wrong
so she gave up

the perfect little house
the perfect little family
that's what my mama always wanted for me
until i lost

but now little miss perfect isn't perfect anymore
little miss perfect's now a shadow on the floor
she's tired
she's crying
she's wondering why
and she doesn't know what to do
an angel sent from hell
in shades of grey and blue

THOSE WALLS

Under starless skies,
lost in the night,
heart of ice,
not melting in the moonlight.
Living in disguise,
buried the pain,
it's the same old story,
but nothing's ever the same.
Every scar on her body,
every story untold,
put the fire out,
now she's feeling cold,
can't trust love, it's let her down before,
she's broken, shattered, invisible tears and a heart once gold.

Memories haunt her, like ghosts in the night,
Once filled with colour, turned black and white,
She put up those walls to hide from the pain,
Are those walls closing in, or is she going insane?

Those walls she built, locked everyone out,

no soul, just ice, no one around,

Numb to the core,

she can't take it anymore,

her warm, brown eyes, have turned to grey,

those walls she built, drove love away.

Under starry skies, I walked alone,

a heart once warm, now turned to stone,

do I still have a soul, or is it just ice and frost,

under starless skies, I walk alone, wandering and lost.

Those walls that I've built, that I can't seem to break down,

in the deepest oceans I swam, but in this mirage, I drown...

NOT A CRY FOR HELP

In the heart of the city where lights they dance bright,
There's a soul wandering, lost in the night.
Not a cry for help, just a whisper in the dark,
Like a lone wolf howling, searching for a spark.

I'm the echo in the canyon, barely heard,
Not a cry for help, just a whispered word.
Lost in the crowd, like a grain of sand,
But I'm not waving hands, just holding my stand.

In the chaos of the city, I'm a passing car,
Not a cry for help, just a fading star.
A melody in silence, barely sung,
But I'm not seeking rescue, just biting my tongue.

Like a shadow in the dusk, I blend in,
Not a cry for help, just a silent spin.
A ripple in the ocean, unnoticed by sight,
But I'm not reaching out, just staying out of the fight.

I'm the ink on the page, unread and unseen,
Not a cry for help, just a girl who wants to be seen.
A whisper in the wind, easily missed,
But I'm not seeking solace, just existing in the mist.

So just don't let me fade into the background, and don't make a fuss,

Not a cry for help, just a passing hush.

A grain of sand on the shore, swept away,

But I'm not asking for rescue, just another day.

Roses have
thorns that
leave scars.

"Et tu, Brute?"

Sir William Shakespeare
Julius Caesar, Act 3, Scene 1

Dear Reader,

"Betrayal is the one truth that sticks." A part of life is facing disappointment, having your trust shattered—often by those you thought would be with you forever. Betrayal is like being in a dream, only to be jolted awake by the realization that someone you believed in didn't believe in you. Someone you cared deeply for didn't care for you. What you'd have done for them; they wouldn't have done for you. Betrayal is when you live your life in disillusionment and when you finally snapped back to reality, you realize that your feelings went unreciprocated, left unrequited.

But as I've said before, 'If they leave, they were never yours to begin with.'

I won't tell you to let it go, or to get over it. But I will tell you, to feel that pain and, to let it drive you to places you couldn't even dream of before.

It's okay to be hurt, as long as you don't let it swallow you whole.

Love, T.

BETRAYED

In shadows cast by counterfeit smiles,
A dance of lies, friendship beguiles.
In whispers masked, deceit compiles,
Each bond a facade, the truth defiles.

In hearts once warm, betrayal's sting,
Like serpents coiled, a venomous thing.
With every kiss, a viper's fling,
Leaves wounds that ache, silent zing.

Lost in the labyrinth of despair,
Where shattered dreams hang in the air.
Hope's fading ember, beyond repair,
A spectre haunting, relentless glare.

Amidst the maze of fractured self,
Identity adrift, seeking stealth.
A puzzle unsolved, a book on a shelf,
Unravelling secrets, hidden wealth.

In solitude's embrace, I roam,
An exile from the world, my home.
A wanderer in the vast unknown,
Seeking solace where seeds are sown.

IT'S OKAY

It's okay

I know it was meant to end sometime

It's okay I knew it all along, I'm fine

It's okay, now I know best-friends don't always stay for life.

Did you really have to leave me when I needed you most?

Were you happy when I said goodbye, because I was lost

Did you throw a party,

Or did you raise a toast?

It's okay

It was expected along, it's me who always gets left

But now you're changed - superficial and no fun

Fake smiles, shallow laughs, what have you done?

It's okay, it really is hard to believe that everything happens for the best.

It's okay, you're pretending to like the music they like

It's okay, I'm no longer your kryptonite

It's okay, no matter how much I expect disappointment, I still get disappointed

It's okay, I'm not that girl anymore who told you to stay and fight.

It's okay

You've left me for them,

Who'll leave you the same way you left me,

And you'll miss the Saturday nights you spent at my place,

You'll regret obsessing over a girl who lied to your face,

and ditching me for a boy who liked me instead

So, it's okay.

Something untrue is bound to end.

It's okay.

Because you were always the fake friend.

AN ANGEL SENT FROM HELL

Drama, hurt and friendships fake
Pain, betrayal and heartache
Haste, desire, for who's sake
Jealousy, obsession, leaving all at stake
Enchantments of liking, remain unknown
Lonely days, yet not alone
Questions raised, in a craving tone
Insecurities and acceptance, all turned to stone
Demons and angels quarrelling within
The tyranny of the heart must begin
The angels forgoing every sin
Yet, neither the angel nor the devil win...

Inception & butterflies

"All we see or seem is but a dream within a dream"

Edgar Alla Poe

Dear Reader,

Have you ever wondered if everything was just a dream? If you are actually a butterfly imagining life as a human. If you wake up, and you're a completely different person. If everything was a dream, if you could go back in time, would you still be you? Would you want to change?

I wouldn't. I have joyful moments, and I have sorrowful ones. But I wouldn't trade them for anything in the world. I wouldn't because, every single second of my life has made me who I am today; and as flawed as I am, those flaws are what make me beautiful, that make me, me, and I rather like that person.

So, even if it is all a dream; even if you are a butterfly, don't give up and certainly don't undermine your worth. Because I know for a fact, that who you think you are is who you become.

Love, T.

INCEPTION

I'm up at night, it's the insomnia
A thought lost in the maze or a crazy idea
I stare at a ceiling too dark to see
I wonder of a future and what it may be

Maybe I am but a dream, a figment of some mind
Or perhaps I'm just a butterfly, fluttering to find
A reality within a dream, a dream within a mind
Asking questions to which answers I will never to find

Do the stars really wink, or is it merely a game?
Does the fame come with spotlight, or spotlight with fame?
If I'm a dream, who's dreaming me?
Another butterfly or just a fantasy?

Its 3AM, I wonder who to be
What's the best way to hide a body?
Fulfil expectations, get a fancy degree
Is it really that horrific, being ordinary?

They feel sorrow, when they see a bird that's caged
The feel pity, when they see a tigress that's aged
They feel fear after a thunderstorm that's raged
Is it really true, or is it just a play that's been staged?

It really is inception that kills you

Or is it the curiosity that runs wild when there's nothing better to do?

The question really is "is it all true?"

But these questions don't have answers, for nobody has a clue!

THE DECEASED

In the quiet night, under starlit sky,
I think about the ones who said goodbye.
Forever, they rest, in lands unknown,
Yet their whispers linger, in my heart, they've grown.

The living, they expect, they have their demands,
But pleasing them? I try, with the cards in my hand.
I try my best, but it's never enough,
I try my best, but even I've got my stuff.

The dead, they watch from their ethereal perch,
Do they judge? Or do they simply search?
For something greater, beyond earthly grind,
A soul's true essence, to which they're aligned.

But here I am, struggling to please,
The living's wishes, like a ship on rough seas.
Their expectations tower like mountains tall,
While I stumble and falter, feeling small.

I chase their approval, like a dog with a bone,
But it slips away, leaving me alone.
For the dead, though gone, they still hold sway,
Their legacy haunting my every day.

So, I'll carry on, amidst this strife,
Trying to navigate this maze called life.
Perhaps one day, I'll find my stride,
And make the deceased proud, with nothing to hide.

WAR

The holocaust in Germany
Endless destruction till '43
Discrimination, hate, jealousy
This became the new reality
Men, women & children died
Many tried to run and hide
Enemies that were on their side
Shattered them, so they never tried
Bloodthirsty rivers
Merciless murders
Gunshots & quivers
Memories that bring shivers
The world is not what it should be
Why can't they open their eyes and see
That happiness is the key
And peace is not to be sold, but free
Why this destruction, why this agony
Those memories are a felony
The bigotry is an irony
What is equality?
Innocent souls lost to the flames
Their cries echoing in history's frames

Silenced voices, forgotten names
Their suffering, the world defames
Ashes scattered, a haunting sight
Darkness descended, obscuring the light
In the midst of horror, still, they fought to unite
For freedom, for justice, for what's right
In camps they suffered, lost and scared
Their voices silenced, nobody cared
Inhumanity beyond compare
Leaving scars that never repaired
Tales of horror echo still
Survivors' voices, a haunting chill
Their stories, a testament, a will

-July 11, 2021
(11 years old)

WHEN I'M 25

When I'm 25
I want pretty hair
I want to live life as though it were a dare
I want to have another book out
A bestseller that everyone's raving about
When I'm 25
I want that little apartment that I've imagined in my head
Probably even dye my hair, blue or green or red
I want a purple guitar and a grey wall just for paintings
I want to buy my mom a pair of diamond earrings
When I'm 25
I want to laugh until my stomach aches
cry my eyes out, stuff myself with cake
I want to feel like I can fly
Want to be able to paint the world, the trees, the sky
When I'm 25
I'm going to be me living my life
Maybe still cut my finger with a knife
sit on my couch, pasta and red wine
I want to have a world that I can call mine
When I'm 25
I want to be able to look 13 year old me in the eye
tell her with confidence and head held high
"Honey look, we turned out fine
Don't you worry, it'll be alright

WHY?

why does the sun rise in the east
why does the moon wax and wane
why do we laugh when we're happy
why do we cry when we're in pain
why do birds sing in the morning
why do stars twinkle at night
why does love always hurt
why does darkness run from light
why do oceans kiss the shore
why do rivers flow and bend
why do trees whisper secrets
why do storms come to an end
why do dreams seem so real
why do nightmares haunt our sleep
why do memories fade away
why do we make promises we can't keep
why do flowers bloom in spring
why do leaves shed in the fall
why do lies come so easy
why does my truth make no sense, not even a little, not even at all
why does the heart ache with the past and pretence
why does life go on without consequence

why did I chase a dream, so out of reach
why does the sun set in the west and not the east
why did I forget to live, to truly be alive...
some questions don't have answers, to each and every why
thus, c'est la vie that's life, that's why.

The clearer the mirror, the more it stings.

"In me she has drowned a young girl, and in me an old woman rises toward the day after day, like a terrible fish."

Sylvia Plath, Mirror

Dear Reader,

Sometimes you may feel like the world is trying to change you because no matter what you do, you could never fulfil their expectations. You're always 'almost there'. Just half an inch away. You look at yourself in the mirror, and you despise what you see. You want to live up to society's expectations; you're sacrificing your food as well as your happiness. You have to look perfect, dress perfect, act perfect. But what is 'this' perfect? Is 'perfect' fitting into a pair of size 0 jeans? Being that 'it' girl with her cutesy clothes, bows and demure persona? Faking smiles and stifling vivaciously beautiful laughs just to dodge their disapproving glares? Starving yourself so that your body fits their definition of conventional? But shouldn't 'perfect' be, living how you want to live? What's wrong in being a little bit curvy and having a bubbly laugh that might sound like a goat bleating if it makes you happy?

As I pen these words of wisdom, I feel like a BIG BIG BIG hypocrite. Why? Because I don't love me for me. Because I don't like what I see in the mirror. Because I absolutely loathe my body. I detest who I was and I'm struggling terribly, to find out who I am. While my words may sound deprecating to you, either you relate to them or you once did.

I don't know much, but I do know that I will vanquish this, and then I will have truly grown up.

So, I'm not going to give you advice, rather I will give you hope, that it will all be okay.

Love, T.

I'M STILL ME

They say "you're this", they say "you're that"
They say "you're too thin", "you're too fat"
They try to box me, give me a label and define
But you see, I'm not a category, I am not a sign.
I was lost in their words, almost forgot who I am
It took some time,
but then it hit me
I'm the same, I'm still me
And then they said "we owe you an apology
But what good would that be?
And I go to the mirror, smile, and see,
I may be lost,
but I'm still me.

IMPERFECTLY PERFECT

Why do you think that you're always right?
Why can't you live without a fight?
Why do you have to do this every time?
And if i'm such a "good-for-nothing"
Why can't you stop cribbing?
What's wrong if my words rhyme?
If you really want me to "go to hell"
Then keep doing what you do,
Go ahead, yell
Go ahead, call me a loser,
Call me mentally unfit,
Go ahead, say that i'm not worth it
I know i'm not perfect
I'm not always right
But how do you know for sure that i'm not worth it
It's just me, it's just how i am
I want to be me, be who i want to be
But you really need to lower the bar for me
Because i'm just human,
I fall, i stumble, i'm not wonder woman
So, drop it or fix it, because i really am tired.
I'm perfectly imperfect, come on i want to see those insults you so desperately wanted to see fired
So just stop.

MAMA'S EYES

Why does the heart break into another tiny piece in front of the mirror?

Is it vanity or hope because only the glass gets clearer?

Why does the heart ache in the prospect of not being me?

In a crowd of thousands, why does the heart still feel lonely?

What is it with us? our face, our body, is never enough

To compare constantly with beauty and insecurities, isn't it tough?

And sometimes all I wish for is my mama's eyes

Because then my beauty will be the truth and my eyes will speak lies

So, I wish for mama's eyes, pray the pain goes away

I wish for mama's eyes, to be as pretty as dandelions in may

I wish for mama's eyes, so I can be my first love

I wish for mama's eyes, so I'm finally enough.

METAMORPHOSIS

That night, I cried, when it rained
That night, I cried, because it all pained
That night, I cried, I finally knew
That the only thing that's killing me, is you
And I thought to myself, what good is it?
Writing page after page at 3 AM?
But hurts so much because...

That day, I spent, sitting on the beach
That day, I spent, with reality out of reach
That day, I spent, it's the happiest I've been in a year
That day, I spent, I let it all go, the pain, the fear
But that day was too short
And it hurts because...

I went from "I want to be a grownup"
To "I want to be a kid again"
From "no one can tell me what to do"
To "please help me, I'm in pain"
From being the happiest kid ever
To "I'm tired of faking it"
From "scream at me all you want, but don't hit me please"

To "just don't say a word, I'd rather get hit"
From crying my eyes out till they turn red
To "I've run out of tears and I'd rather cry instead"

I went from being a genius
To a burnt-out star
To someone who barely makes it
From someone who would set the bar
From that happy little kid
To someone lost in the in-between
From someone who lived for the spotlight
To barely wanting to be seen
From someone who spent her days laughing
To someone who spends her nights in agony
I went from being "little miss perfect"
To just being me.

TEARDROPS ON MY GUITAR

Sitting in the corner of my room
Lost under the fairy lights, can't smile but can't cry either
Like that flower that doesn't wilt but neither does it bloom

I'm upset, not because of what he did,
Not because there's always something up,
But because I'm either an adult or just a little kid

And so, I'm sitting on the floor
Staring at my cream-coloured wall
Thinking too much, but feeling nothing at all
Guitar rested on my thigh
Just know when I say that I'm okay, it's always a lie

So, I'm sitting on the floor, staring at the wall
Hoping that I stumble but don't ever fall
Guitar on my thigh, pen in my hand

Everyone around me disappearing like footprints on sand
I'm just so tired, but I can't sleep
And I'm sinking in waters that aren't even deep
I'm too afraid to try, so I look from afar
Pouring my pathetic heart out, wiping teardrops off my guitar...

It's just so hard to deal with everything
either it's all or nothing
"I'm too fat, I'm too thin", but I'm never right
Sometimes I just want to give up, and not fight

And when I look in the mirror, all I see are flaws
I can't help but wonder if you see them too
And when I look in the mirror,
I can't help but wonder what it would be like to be you.

And so, I'm just sitting in the corner of my room
Staring at my cream-coloured wall
Sinking in waters that just aren't deep, at all
Pen in my hand, head in the stars
Wiping each teardrop off my guitar
And I wonder when we look in the mirror, why do we see someone who's never good enough?
Tell me why when you look in the mirror, you see someone you can't truly love?
And so, as I drown, and as I sink
There's just one thing I want you to think
Will we ever be good enough?
In the mirror will we ever see someone we truly love?
So, society, I beg you, lower the bar
As I wipe each teardrop off my guitar.

WAISTLINE

What does it matter if I was a size 26

What does it matter if I was as thin as sticks

What does it matter if I don't fit in my jeans that were a 28

What does it matter if in this last year I put on a little weight

Isn't it better than starving my body until I collapse

Not being able to think straight

Because I threw up everything I ate

And I can't exercise, it hurts too much, it's the déjà vu

Of when my body was perfect according to you,

When I fit into your standards that just don't seem to work out for me

Because I can't take it anymore, let me be.

What does it matter if your ideals seem cruel,

When my worth is not measured by a number or a rule?

What does it matter if I don't conform to their mould,

When beauty lies in confidence and being bold?

Isn't it better to embrace my curves and my flaws,

Than to chase an image that constantly withdraws?

To nourish my body, mind, and soul,

And reject what's meant to be my societal role

That I must shrink myself to fit your narrow view,
For my worth is not defined by what you construe.
My worth won't be buried like footprints in the sand
What does it matter if your standards fail to see,
The beauty that resides in uniqueness, in being free?
Why should I conform to a standard that's not my own,
When who I am is not defined by a number or a tone?

So, what if I'm not a size that fits their narrow view,
So, what if I do what I want to do?
For I am more than a number, more than what meets their gaze,

I am a me, forever and always.
So, stand beside me or step out of my way
Because your ideas don't matter to me, anyway.

A broken clock

"Sorrow is knowledge: they who know the most must mourn the deepest o'er the fatal truth, the Tree of Knowledge is not that of Life"

Lord Byron

Dear Reader,

Sorrow, that relentless shadow, never fails to intrude unbidden. It is almost artful, the way it slips into the cracks of your seemingly steady resolve, just as you dare to believe you've pieced it all together. It envelops you like a damp, suffocating mist, seeping into your very core, whispering haunting refrains of despair. How meticulous it is in cataloguing every misstep and regret, ensuring none escape your notice—as though you might dare to forget. And the tears, though they pour freely, offer no solace, merely the illusion of relief, a cruel parody of healing. Sorrow—a tireless spectre, perfectly attuned to the moment of its intrusion, yet hopelessly ignorant of when it should finally take its leave. I have seen sorrow; enough of it to know that it is imperative to feel sorrow, to truly experience joy.

Without sorrow, there is no joy; and without joy, there is no sorrow.

In this Lord Byron was true, sorrow truly is knowledge.

Love, T.

CRY ME RIVER

Cry me a river
To wash away the pain
Cry me a river
So i'll never cry again
Cry me a river
While i'm standing in the rain
Cry me a river
So no one will know this stain
Cry me a river
Spare no effort to stay sane
Cry me a river
So the struggle won't go in vain
Cry me a river
The illusion will begin to wane
Cry me a river
So my sunshine beams again
Cry me a river
Beneath the moon's soft glow
Cry me a river
Where tears and time flow
Cry me a river
Where whispers fade to sigh
Cry me a river
As old wounds start to die

Cry me a river
In the quiet of the morn
Cry me a river
Where new dreams are born
Cry me a river
Let the tears fall like rain
Cry me a river
So I'm finally whole again
Cry me a river, so i never cry again

EPIPHANY

"My heart it's small

How can it carry so much sorrow?

he asked

"But my eyes, they're so small

Yet they behold the world"

he spoke

But doesn't it hurt, to carry something so heavy, in something so small?

Isn't it better to feel nothing at all?

Isn't it better to run from the pain?

Isn't it better to dance instead of cry in the rain?

Isn't it better to be empty instead of hurting?

Is a flood better than to watch the city burning?

Is there choice, or is there just way?

Is the night more beautiful, or is it day?

Is it better for the villain to have face?

Does it all even matter in the first place?

DÉJÀ VU

It's just this time of the year, right?

When all of it goes dark, oblivious to the light.

Is it just me? Is this how it'll always be?

I'm not blind, it's just the hope that I can't see.

Maybe it could all just be a dream.

I hope so, but the hope is gone, and all I can do is scream.

They say life's not just black and white, and that colour really does exist.

But the colour is gone, there's just shades of grey.

I can't feel it at all, it's an endless list.

When it all finally seems to become alright,

Just like last year, it'll break and fall to pieces again, and I won't be able to shed a tear.

I knew it all along, I knew this would happen all over again.

And all I know now, is that I won't be able to wash away this pain.

Just like last year, I hope I sleep through the night, so I wake up to finally see the light.

And just like last year, it'll break and fall to pieces again, but I won't need to shed a tear.

Because I knew it would happen, and I knew it would be alright someday.

Because life's not just black and white, there's always shades of grey.

It's just this weird feeling of Deja vu,

I can't hide it any longer, that's just what I can't do.

They say give up before it gets too late,

and that life's going to be hard, but honey, it's just fate.

And when you're flying high, you're bound to fall,

they're going to make you feel like you're nothing at all.

So, it's just this time of the year, right?

Because just like last year,

it'll break and fall to pieces again, and this time, I won't be able to shed a tear.

UNTITLED

Was four years really not enough?

Do you really have to twist the story, make it so tough?

Do you not see that I'm in pain?

Why do you have to do this, I don't understand?

Fine, victimize yourself, tell them that it's all my fault

Because they'll never know what happens behind closed doors, so go ahead if that's what you want.

So why don't you go and pretend like the amazing, Samaritan that you are

While I shed tears that I don't have any more and cry to someone who's long been a star

I have one request though, just one

Don't kill someone who's trying her best just to feel that you've won

And don't make it any harder than it already is,

Because if it weren't for you, it would've never come to this.

WE'LL BOTH DIE

Is all you know, only how to hurt?

Does all this that you do, really have any worth?

You know what you are, now I know too

That if there's anyone on earth, synonymous to Satan, it's you.

You know you're a liar, a damned cheat

You disgust me more than ever, so much so, that my heart's lost its beat

You're an egotist, a narcissist, a hypocrite, inhuman

You think you're better than everyone, when in fact you really are no one

You thought you could be sweet as poison, right to my face

Sharpen your knives behind my back, just to cut to the chase

You made me cry tears of blood; you think you're the best thing for me

But you're the reason I'm broken, shattered, lost all faith to be

You think you can hurt the one person I love most, and I'll still like you after it all

You caused me pain, you're a sadist, the reason I never call

So get over your damn self and stop torturing her till she gives up

Give me back my life, my hope, my strength to fight when it gets tough

And if you have to kill anyone, really it should be me

Because after all I'm the problem, right?

Stop trying to make yourself feel better by picking up just another fight

So, treat her with respect, because she really did nothing to deserve all this

She's infinitely better than you are,

The only victim in our cold war

So if there's anyone you have to kill, kill me

Because it really is me who's the problem right?

Don't shout at her to save your fragile ego, and don't you dare pick up another fight

I won't tell you to die or her to calm down

Just know there will be blood on my hands, if you keep me around

So leave me be, for we both will face our end

You're a sadist, an egoist, with not one true friend.

I'M NOT FINE?

Why is it that I keep getting sucked in, when what I crave most I to be left out?

Why is it that even when it's not my fault, it's my name that you scream and shout?

Why is it that even though it was no choice of mine,

It's me standing here in purgatory, claiming that I'm fine?

Why is it that it's me who's alone, when it was me who tried to be nice first?

Why is it that it's just me who in the drought couldn't quench her thirst?

Why is it that Earth has turned to hell, before it was ever my truth?

Why is it that after all this pain, you blame me when I'm rude and uncouth?

Why is that in a world where hearts beat, mine was coerced to a halt?

Why is it that even when I tried my best, on my wounds you rubbed salt?

Why is it that in your game of 'tug of war' you've made me the rope?

Why is it that it's just me from whom you've stolen all hope?

Why is it that after all of this, I don't know who to blame or why?

Why is it that none of my oceans can spare me just a tear to get by?

Why is it that after everything, you still can't see what you did wrong?

Why is it that your heart's weak, but your ego still stands strong?

Why is it that you get the luxury to say your pride is fragile?

Why is it that no matter how hurt mine is, all you ask for is the data points and smile?

Why is it that after it all you are still blinded to why in the end you will lose?

Why is it that after it all no one seems to care about how broken I am or how bruised?

Why is it that they let murderers like you roam free on the street?

You killed me, killed my spirit, killed my heart so it'll never beat.

WONDER

I wonder, what it would be like in a world where I don't say "I'm just so tired of life"

And I wonder, what it would be like in a world where I don't say "I want to live and not just survive"

And I wonder, what it would be like in a world where I don't say

"I know I'm legally not allowed to drive yet, but I just want to speed off the highway"

And I wonder, what it would be like in a world where I don't say "I don't want to live like the living dead"

And I wonder, what it would be like in a world where I don't say "I don't ever want to get out of bed"

And I wonder, what it would be like in a world where I don't say

"You're right, life's not always black & white, there's always shades of grey"

I don't just want to wonder, I want to live

Is the pain really all that we have left to give?

Does it always have to be this way?

I know that world will never come

There's no point in wondering, so I'm just done.

Maybe I'll just hope that this pain goes away?

Caught in the in-between, don't know which way to go

Is this confusion or pain, I've never felt this way before

I'm guessing I'm just lost in the middle, can't find my way

I break and I fall, as night turns to day...

And I wonder, what it would be like in a world where I don’t say "why don’t they ever seem to understand?"

And I wonder, what it would be like in a world where I don’t say "I don’t want to live, but I don't want to die"

And I wonder, what it would be like in a world where I don’t say "don’t they know, you can only give up, if you ever tried"

So, I just wonder.

IS IT JUST ME?

You hit me with the knife

Beat me up - and you said get a life

You said I was worthless anyway

Left me crying in the middle of the street - then drove away

You made me cry, but I still tried, for you

Now you're screaming and shouting, is that all you can do?

So tell me why, was it meant to be this way?

Is it just me? or is 'loser' all you can say?

Is it just me feeling this pain?

is it just me drowning in the rain?

Is it just me down heartbreak lane?

Is it just me or are your lies insane?

Is it just me or did someone make you this way?

Is it just me or did you not have a heart in the first place?

Is it just me or are you a hypocrite?

Is it just me or are you the one who's "mentally unfit"?

Is it just me or is this really pain?

Is it just me standing in the rain?

Is it just me, am I going insane?

The glass isn't half empty, neither is it half full, it's just shattered.

"The secret of happiness, you see is not found in seeking more, but in developing the capacity to enjoy less."

Socrates

Dear Reader,

'You hope for things, you get disappointed.' This is what I've seen. Disappointment is inevitable if you have hope. It's truly sad really, everything is so black and white that we miss the shades of grey. The emotion. The colour. There's too much that's beautiful and yet we only catch a tiny glimpse of it. I've come to the realization that lowering our expectations often leads to greater contentment. The more deeply we invest in caring, the more room we leave for disappointment. I'm torn between daring to hope and accepting the inexorable disillusionments, or simply tempering my hopes from the beginning. All I do know, is that regardless of the outcome I must confront it.

So dear reader, no matter what happens in life, you have no choice but to face it. Life isn't a multiple-choice test; your answers can only be subjective.

Love, T.

NYCTOPHILIA

It's beautiful isn't it
In a way we never realize
It's beautiful isn't it
No pollution, no lies
It's beautiful isn't it
They way the stars light up the skies
It's beautiful isn't it
The moon and fireflies
It's beautiful isn't it
How it’s never the same
It's beautiful isn't it
all of it in one frame
And really, what a pity it is
For no one ever sees its beauty
The moonlight, the waves
The nighttime sea
It really is prettier than golden and blue
A beauty it is isn't it, one that's true

SCARED OF DARK

Where do the lies end, and the truth begin?
When will I go from being alive, so start living?
Why are those windows tinted?
Why is that movie black and white?
I didn't see it coming, as day turned to night.
What is this cruelty?
Life without consequence?
This heart of stone-
Surrounded by a white, picket fence.
So, Why are you scared of the dark?
Are you running out of light?
But the light's too bright, for me to survive.
Why are you scared of the dark?
Why do you need the light?
The light just blinds you, so the stars are out of sight.
Why are you scared of the dark?
Are you scared of what you can't see?
But the dark is so beautiful, for it hides the pain and the misery.
Why are you scared of the dark?
Are you running out of light?
But the light just blinds the beauty of the night.

GOOD TIMES

I shouldn't miss the high tide
After being the reason, the ocean went dry
I shouldn't be stuck in delusion
It's my fault I'm the villain, I can't ask why
I remember the feeling, when I realized the earth revolves around the sun
When I first learnt that in 1000 years even the sun can burn out
I never knew that the moon's light wasn't its own
But now that I know suddenly I'm filled with doubt
Is it wrong to miss the sun when it sets
After complaining of the heat all day
Is it wrong to wish for the night to not end
Is it wrong to for once, go the easy way
Isn't it wrong to say it's a thunderstorm, but treat it like a drizzle
Isn't it wrong to say that it was just rain
Isn't it wrong to miss the wave
Isn't it wrong to wish there was a tsunami again.
Was it fun? To give me hope just to take it away
Was it fun? To make me feel like I was flying just to push me to the ground?
Was it fun? To give me my first love just to make me hate it with the fire of 1000 suns
Was it fun? To strip me of my good times just to lock me in this hellhound?

IT'S STILL PRETTY

When you wore a tiara, I wore headphones
When you wore mascara, I wore my glasses
And that was all I needed
When you wore high-heels, I wore sneakers
When you scrolled through reels, I turned pages
And that was how I rolled
When you went out partying, I stayed home and read
When you were dreaming, I had nightmares
And that's just how it was
Because I was just there, trying to be me
When you were all, I ever wanted to be
But I couldn't, and that's just how it was
And I get it now how you wanted me to see
That life may not be beautiful, but it's still pretty
We both know that everything always went your way
When for me, luck was just walking away
You'd think I was jealous, because your life looked pretty and perfect on the outside
While everyone saw my broken home and the shattered glass scattered inside
Your world was gold, your life a dream
But I was never jealous
How could I be, after all we were the same

When you got a boyfriend, and I was just there

I said "if you hurt her, you'll end up dead"

After everything, I was the disappointment, the bad one,
is that fair?

When all I was trying to do, was do just what I said

And that's when it hit me, like a bullet to the heart

I started to get, what you meant, when you said,

"Life may not be beautiful, but it's still pretty".

The price you pay when you shine.

"Some people try to destroy you, precisely because they recognize your power—not because they don't see it, but because they see it and they don't want it to exist."

– bell hooks

Dear Reader,

The brilliance of something rare often draws envy from those who cannot fathom its radiance. Like stars punctuating the night, luminescent against the vast darkness, those who dare to shine find themselves targets of resentment. Like moths drawn to flame, people are both mesmerized and threatened by those who dare to shine. Rocks—harsh words, disdainful looks, malicious actions—are hurled at the luminous, not because they are flawed, but because their radiance exposes the shadows and inadequacy of the dim. It's a bitter irony: what captivates is also what evokes resentment. But such is the nature of light—it does not dim to accommodate the comfort of those still dwelling in darkness. Instead, it persists, undeterred, knowing that true brilliance is often met with the sharpest resistance.

Disclaimer! I don't mean to compare myself to the luminescent, quite far from it actually. All I've said is purely an observation, not intended to hurt, harm or offend any individual.

Love, T.

GOSSIP

How is it that he gets to manipulate the situation

How is it that he gets to deny everything, call it my imagination

Why does he get to lie and twist the story, make it all my fault

But it is isn't it, I should've just ignored the humiliation and assault

But really, what does it matter right?

Because who wants to see a 10-year-old girl put up a fight

All you want is the free entertainment

And you think that the truth is just the story that you've created

And I really don't care if you think that he wasn't wrong

Who are you to judge anyway, when you know nothing at all?

Are you really that vain,

that you get a high out of my pain?

So, to all of you who wasted 4 years talking about me

Did you really have nothing better to do, perhaps discuss war or read poetry?

And let's face it, there's just one reason that you spoke about me

Because if you spoke about yourself, they would walk away and leave you be

So, my dear gossip mongers living across the street
Instead of discussing me, try and make yourself worthy
And I really do wish you luck, I really do
Because it's not me who needs it but you...

PETULANCE

In a garden you see, there lies a petulance,
A stubborn seed that sprouts defiance, sans any semblance,
It grows unchecked, a tangled vine of discontent,
Its roots deep-seated, its thorns a constant torment.
With every ray of sun, it flourishes with might,
Feeding on grievances, basking in its spite,
No gentle rain can quench its thirst for ire,
No whispered plea can douse its raging fire.
It coils around my thoughts, choking out the light,
Its tendrils twisting, turning day into night,
It whispers doubts and fears, a relentless refrain,
A symphony of bitterness, a never-ending pain.
I try to prune it back, to tame its wild ways,
But it laughs in defiance, mocking my futile gaze,
For in this garden of mine, it reigns supreme,
A petulant reminder of what might have been.
So, I learn to live with it, this thorn in my side,
A constant companion on this tumultuous ride,
For sometimes, in the darkness, it whispers truths untold,
A bitter pill to swallow, a story yet to unfold.
And though I may resent it, this petulance within,
I know it's just a part of me, a shadow, a twin,
So, I'll tend to my garden, despite its thorny fence,
And learn to coexist with my own petulance.

THE CLIMB

A will, a desire,
An ambition, a fire
To excel among the best,
To shine beyond the rest.
Disappointments, tear-stained eyes,
Judgments, experiences, size.
Normal, usual, words unknown,
Anger, fury, emotions not shown.
Many fell in the tempest's might,
She lingered, striving for the light.
Struggling to rise from the ground,
While others wept, she made no sound.
Humility engraved deep within,
A smile emerged from a frown's thin.
While others slept through the night,
She toiled on, her struggle tight.
It ended with her at the peak,
Fame, success, yet she stayed meek.
Though battles raged, her sight was clear,
Ambition drove her, year after year.
Giving up was not her way,
Winning was her word to stay.

-21/11/2021
(11 years old)

TEENAGE DREAM

Summertime skies, basking in sunlight,
Kicking back, feeling free, everything's just right.
Sneakers on the sidewalk, the world at our feet,
Dreams in our pockets, hearts with a beat.
Late-night whispers on the phone,
Secrets and stories, we're never alone.
Laughter echoing in the breeze,
Carefree days, we do as we please.
Sneaking out past midnight's call,
Climbing fences, risking it all.
Moonlit roads, adventures untold,
The stories we'll tell when we're old.
Faded jeans and worn-out tees,
Music loud, we're living for moments like these.
Dancing like nobody's there,
In our own world, without a care...
Bonfire nights and stargazing dreams,
Life's a whirlwind, or so it seems.
But these days, they're ours to keep,
In our hearts, forever deep.
Chasing sunsets, racing dawn,
Living fast, until they're gone
It's a Teenage dream, wild and free,
In this moment, we're who we're meant to be.

The unsung ballad...

"We don't read and write poetry because it's cute. We read and write poetry because we are members of the human race.

And the human race is filled with passion. Medicine, law, business, engineering—these are noble pursuits and necessary to sustain life. But poetry, beauty, romance, love—these are what we stay alive for."

John Keating,
Dead Poets Society (1989)

Dear Reader,

The following pieces of poetry, truly speaking, are lyrical in nature. Their genesis took place on my bedroom floor with scattered paper, a rusty guitar, and an archaic piano. I think it's safe to say that this bouquet preceding you, is the most cherished to me. Maybe because they are fairly recent (as of 1.11.2025) or because they stemmed from melody. Regardless, I find that there is more me in these pages then there was in the rest of this book.

I hope that my words incite some emotion in you. It doesn't matter which, all that matters is that it is yours. Unique to you. The beautiful thing about poetry, is how iridescent it is. Every piece of poetry is anamorphic. Perspectives are subjective and arise on the basis of the eyes of its beholder. I do not wish that you be inundated by my words, all that I want, is that you feel them. Feel them beneath your skin, in the marrow of your bones, in every fibre of your being. Just feel.

So, I will leave you to it, and bid you adieu.

Love, T.

THIRTEEN

I left it all and I ran away
Thought it'd be better this way
You kick me out, then you crawl back in
I never should've let you win
You say that you like me now
God, how pathetic is that
You're just a little too late
I've come a long way since I was eight.
Thirteen wasn't lucky to you, but it was, to me
I was just a loser to you, but I wasn't, to me
And now I'm trying.
I'm trying to get to every piece
Running, running, running
With screwed up knees.

SWEATERS IN JULY

And I'm wearing sweaters in July
Wrapped in my head
I'm wondering why
Too tired to say goodbye
Oh, I try, Oh I try, Oh I try, Oh I try
I give it all, just to survive
Oh, what it is to live,
But I'm just alive.
Take me home, get me out of here
Take me home, make me disappear
Take me home, before I float away
Take me home, before I die -
Anyway.

DREAMS

Dreams turn to nightmares
The silence feels carnivorous
Your sanctimony still echoes
Locked me in a cage
You're poisonous
Indoctrination stains me
I'm burnt by their decree
The sermons are chloroform
I've lost to what could be
I gave you all my secrets
They dissolved into the sea
You wrote your name in embers
And it branded over me
You smiled like it was holy
As the stars fell out of view
Grabbed the knife
Just as I turned my back to you

BLUE

You said blue looked prettier when it was on me
Like the sky right before it starts to bleed
Picasso, you painted my dreams
Now she's all that you see
Took the bow from my hair
Translucent black with a little twist
You never gave it back
I didn't ask
You kept it like a secret in your jacket clasp
You kept us like a secret when we fell back.

YOUR EYES ON MINE

You lean in just a little too close
Like you want to say my name
I caught your gaze when I shouldn't
Your eyes still trace where mine have been

Do you love me in the silence?
Do you hate me in the light?
Do you miss me in the spaces
When you run all out of time?

You look at me like I am yours
Then you leave without a word
You said that you loved me once
How did we just crash and burn?

Your hands her skin
Your eyes on mine
Look at me
When you know that I'm not fine
You miss this - we both know it
We were perfect until we weren't
We crashed and we burnt

ALMOST, ALWAYS

I talk in circles just to make you stay
You read the silence
Like it's something that I meant to say
You're the kind of storm
That looks like grace from far away
It wreaks havoc up close
Don't look at me this way
You lower your eyes
Like you're hiding a secret
I trace every word that you say
Like you mean it
You told me that you dreamt of the coast in September
Now it's all that I remember
Anymore.

SAME OLD GAME

I laugh too loud
So, no one asks
If I'm okay
Or why my hands just won't stop shaking
And I burnt another bridge last night
Didn't even watch it fall
What's the point?
I said I wouldn't care
But I do
It's pathetic
I know, I know, I know
You look fine
You're always fine
And I hate it
Or maybe
I hate me more
Because every promise sounds the same
Every ending's just a name
I don't care
You win, I lose
Same old game

LILY

Lily's on my windowsill
Burning in the heat
Paper thin
And trembling
Like the skin around my knees
I'm grappling onto mornings
But they're slipping from my hands
I wake up
Just to lie back down
A body built of sand
The mirror doesn't recognize
The girl it used to frame
Every smile is borrowed
But the heart beats just the same
They let go
Like winter light
Fading from the street
The pieces are all scattered
And so, I'm left incomplete
Lily, everything's on fire
All the rooms I built are empty
The flame is climbing higher

Lily, you're all that I know
I'm ash on the carpet
I'm too tired to let you go
And maybe I was built for breaking
Brittle bones and open hands
Every oath stings like a splinter
Every heartbeat like quicksand
If I'm hard to love,
I'm trying
But trying makes me bleed
Lily, in the smoke I'm reaching
You're all that I need.

THEY DIDN'T TELL ME WHY

They didn't tell me why
The sun refused to shine
In my sky
They didn't tell my why
My stars aren't bright
And they always lie
They didn't tell me why
Every rose that I touched
Would always die
They didn't tell me why
I had to fall
But she got to fly
White picket fences
Perfect lives
Popsicle summers
Winters inside
Spring with the flowers
Fall with the skies
That was the life I,
Lived through my eyes.

WASTED POTENTIAL

I'm ashamed of you
God, you grew up a disaster
What is wrong with you?
Why can't you be a little more like her?
Was all that time that I gave you not enough?
Move on, grow up.
All that wasted potential
Look at the life you threw away
You could've been so much
Now you're just in the way
You used to be brilliant
What got into her?
It's just teenage rebellion
God, that's got to hurt.
What's the point if I'm not getting straight As?
What's the point if I'm not hitting aces?
I'm just a loser
Who couldn't do any better
They're livid because I quit
But it's my fault
They couldn't deal with it.

THE COFFEE'S GONE COLD

The coffee's gone cold
I left it too long
Sitting here, thinking where we went wrong
Tried to move on
That didn't last long
Who would've known
God, I'm not that strong
And I found your sweater in the closet last night
The one I stole because it felt so right
Wore it like armour
It's more like a chain
I can't wash out the scent
I can't shake off the pain
And they say time heals all the cracks
But you're not coming back
Tried drowning it in whiskey
Tried burning all the notes
Didn't want to be a cliché
So, I hate what I wrote
And I wrote you a letter
Which I would never send
But what's the point of an ending

If it all just circles again?

And I don't need a séance

I don't need a goddamn sign

I just want this silence

To feel like it's all mine

I'm tired of lying to myself

I'm tired of living for somebody else

I'm tired

Of doing all of this.

BLUE SCRUNCHIE

I remember when your eyes met mine for the first time
We went from nothing
To fireflies, in the dead of the night
You glanced
Like I was your little secret to keep
You tore us apart
Like promises were cheap
And now you stare like I'm everything
Then leave like it's nothing
Blue scrunchie on your wrist
Blue silence on my lips
Say goodnight at 3 A.M.
Then go and leave me on read
I'm dizzy from the whiplash
But god, I keep coming back
You kept me like a promise in the pocket of your blue jeans
Like they were too heave, too worn, to mean.

DYE

Sitting on the floor
Back against my door
Holding my breath
Till my ribs get sore
I should eat
I should sleep
I should try
Oh, I tried
But my life is a lie
The mirror doesn't help
It just stares right back
Like it knows I won't make it
But it won't tell me that
I want to dye my hair
Baby pink
Make it match, the pills
On the bathroom sink
I want to change it
Like I'm changing the past
Nothing sweet, nothing sweet
Ever lasts
I pull my sweater over my hands

Trace old scars
I don't want to go back
I can't bring myself to do it again
God, I just want it to rain
I tell them I'm okay
I smile on cue
And all I get is
"What the hell went wrong with you?"
So, I'm going to dye my hair
Baby pink
Colour the past
I don't want to think
I'm going to wait for it to rain
Wait for it, to wash away the pain.
I loved you like poetry,
You loved me like war.
I loved you with all of me,
You loved me with nothing at all.

PRETTY LITTLE WAR

1886.

Lace on the battlefield
Heels on the wire
They called her 'darling'
As they lit the pyre
Silhouettes in boardrooms
Not a single face mine
Her no was a whisper
Your yes was a crime
You want a maid,
A virgin,
A whore,
All in one breath
But she's made of spitfire and unpaid debts
You fear what you cage
Then blame it when it bites
She's bled too long
To beg for what's right
She's not your saint
She's not your sin
Not a pretty little war for you to win
I'm not your muse

Not your décor

Not a canvas for your civil war

Not a slave

Not an appendage

They couldn't tame her

So, they locked her in

They paint her in corsets

And tie her down

It's always the lies that drown

Her body's not a metaphor

Her pain's not art

You can't incarcerate her anymore

She's not your broken heart

So, you can go rot in those darkest depths of hell

Scream, and wail, but it's a bottomless well

She can't sit straight for your perfect portrait

An accessory

A trophy

A laurel from society

GOD, JUST END IT.

THE SAME DAMN DAY

We started talking last July
You said you loved my eyes
I guess, that was a lie
We had it all
It was just you and me
It felt like fire underneath our feet
And now she's sitting where I used to sit, next to you
Puts her hair up as she laughs, do you get déjà vu
Her bracelet on your wrist
There's silence on my lips
I'm tired of your games
You ran to her
The same damn day
Why do I trust anything that you say?
No warning, no goodbye
Just her hand in yours
Overnight
Your eyes still wander like before
But you're hers right, sure
And you kissed her lips, the same damn day.

LORE

The start of the finish line is where I run
They see no point if I'm not number one
Bought a ticket to the stars
Now I'm floating, mid-sea
No coast in sight, I'm not who they want me to be
Brushed the dust off dreams they dismissed
I stitched my wounds with what they called "what ifs"
Smile like a secret, eyes like war
You came for the tea, now stay for the lore
Stay for the lore.

CINAMMON TEA

Tell me that you love me
With your voice, like coffee
Tell me that you care
And I'll be yours
Get me lilies
And tell me that you'll never leave
For you I'll tear down my walls
Kisses goodnight
Say that you miss me, every once in a while
Before you came along
I was fine
Loving you is like flowers in June
Salt in the wind,
Watercolour moon
You make me feel like I'm something true
Like I'm beautiful, I'm pretty to you
Your ocean tides and cinnamon tea
Something like poetry reading out to me
And when I said I care
I meant, tread carefully
Because loving you,
Feels a little like loving me.

POKER

We bloomed with the spring, and fell with the fall
Didn't make it past summer, we shattered it all
Your voice was smooth like velvet
Lasted two months but it was epic
I miss when we were us
Winter rolled in and you were icy as hell
I didn't know what changed but I could tell
By the way that you stared
That you still cared
You didn't want to let go
How do you expect for me to read your mind?
Who would've thought I'd be the one you'd find?
Played me like poker
You knew your cards right
They loved your so-called charm – I call bullshit
Tell me that you're here and I'm all in
I tore down my walls and I held on
But you walked away like I was nothing at all.

BARBIE

They pull the strings
Call it debutante grace
Spinning in circles
With a painted- on face
I lost who am
I slipped away
And so, I began to smile
Softened my tongue
Bit back the spite
I was delicate
I was young
But if you take it all away
Then pray, what will be left of me?
All I was
Was a mannequin dressed for vanity
Turn me into a pretty little barbie
Turn me back, then leave me be
Twisted and moulded, stuck pins in my body
Don't tell me to love myself
Stop with the hypocrisy

APATHY

I'd rather you hate me
With passion and with emotion
If you can't ever love me,
I'd rather you hate me
I'd rather you hate me
Because it's empty when there's absolutely nothing
I can't stand the apathy
I'd rather you hate me
I'd rather you hate me
Scream at me, glare at me, denigrate me if you will
Because with you love seems inconceivable, as it should be
I'd rather you hate me
I'd rather you hate me
Because as pathetic as it may sound, without you I am forlorn
You're everything I could want, and more
I'd rather you hate me
I'd rather you hate me
Feel something for me, in any shape, and in any form
The abyss terrifies me
I'd rather you hate me

I'd rather you hate me

Because all that I truly adore, is the idea of a you

I can't stand it, the apathy

I'd rather you hate me

THE GIRL WITH THE MAGIC HAIR

The girl with the magic hair. I have known her. I know her still. She is the girl with the magic hair. My first glimpse of her came scarcely a month after my own birth, and even then, she seemed spun from sunlight itself. She was exquisite, otherworldly, a cascade of molten gold that tumbled down her back, catching the sun, glimmering and bending it to her will.

By the age of four, I was convinced that her golden hair was not henna but enchantment, plucked straight from a fairy tale. She was, in every sense, magical. The lilt of her laughter, the mischievous sparkle in her eyes, the words she spoke that seemed to belong only to her—all of it captivated me. And yet, of all her wonders, the one that truly bewitched me was her smile - slightly crooked, a bright red stain carelessly brushed across her lips. In my imagination, she played across the reels of my mind like a vintage film set to whimsical melody, the world blurring into insignificance, a stage for her and her only.

As I grew, so too did my understanding of the girl with the magic hair. I saw beyond her surface, beyond even the heart that most hold as the measure of a person. Her eyes, once brimming with light, grew heavy from all they had witnessed. Her hands, soft and supple in memory, bore calluses from the life she had meticulously built. And as her skin rippled with the gentle passing of time, she remained achingly beautiful—a beauty so intangible and elusive to the superficial, accessible only to those who have truly lived.

She was, to me, the most human soul conceivable. Wisdom tempered by worry, laughter laced with whimsy. Even at ninety-seven, there remained a girl, a girl with golden hair. The hold she has over me is ineffable. Her perfection lies not in flawlessness but in the seamless union of her imperfections into her virtues—the kindness in her eyes, the familiarity of her smile, the glow of her hair.

She is, and forever will be, the girl with the magic hair.

MONET

I live within myself like a canvas cloaked in a gentle haze, luminous from afar yet trembling with an insidious fatigue that threads itself through every breath I take. It is not the thunderous collapse of ruin, but the slow seep of weariness, inconspicuous to the untrained eye, a quiet undoing that nestles beneath the light. Were I to confess this unraveling, no one would believe me; they would smile with conviction and say, "But you are Monet," as though the name itself were a varnish, a gloss that effaced the fractures beneath. From a distance, I appear like a dream — strokes dissolving into harmony, the suggestion of beauty caught in the soft shimmer of dusk. The panorama is pleasing; it asks nothing more. But approach me closely and the illusion falters. The brushstrokes twist into restless gestures, pigments clot, cracks spread across fragile surfaces, and you see the raw undercurrents that were never meant to be hidden. It is here, in the intimate gaze, that the truth bleeds through: I am not whole, not serene, not untouched by sorrow. Yet what hurts most is not the breaking itself but the abandonment that follows — that no one leans in, no one presses close enough to see me as I am. They are content with distance, content to adore the façade while the pernicious wear gnaws unseen. And so I remain — beautiful from afar, fractured within, the quiet tragedy of a painting mistaken for perfection, effaced by admiration, left aching in solitude.

DEAR DIARY

July 18, 2AM — probably should be sleeping but instead I'm overthinking my coffee intake again.

Today I came to the striking realization that I have an unhealthy attachment to mugs. Not mugs in general — specific ones. Like the pale blue one with a chip on the rim that makes my morning hazelnut latte taste more *poetic.* Or the cutesy one with baby pink hearts that I used to drink hot cocoa from during emotional breakdowns that I called "creative blocks." I swear if someone ever broke one of them, I'd mourn harder than I did my last 'talking stage'.

Anyway, today I cried watching a documentary about trees (yes, trees), because one of them was 600 years old and had never been hugged. Meanwhile I've been hugged 38 times this year and still feel emotionally parched. So maybe I'm the tree. Maybe we're all the tree.

Also, I found comfort in folding laundry today. It's the only time I feel like life has steps that make sense: shirt, fold, stack. If only healing from emotional damage came with an instruction manual.

Okay, I'm going to go spiral in lowercase and pretend I didn't romanticize pain (and maybe even hate) in three different melodies today.

Love,

Me (and my sensitive ceramics)

The End...

ACKNOWLEDGEMENTS

Firstly, I'd like to extend my gratitude to Griffin Publication and Ms. Mousumi Sachdeva for bringing this manuscript to life.

Thank you, ma, for being so accommodating to my crazy writer's block, and random splurges of creativity at the most absurd hours, and most of all, for believing in me, when even I couldn't see any reason to. I love you so much.

Thank you, Nani, for being such an amazing inspiration, and for the writer gene that I've inherited from you.

Thank you, Nani ji, (the girl with the magic hair), for being my muse, my storyteller, and my human google.

To Vivi, Aana, and Sid, for being the most chaotic but somewhat loveable and downright amazing best friends ever.

To Lotus-Potus, and my wise, old, Gin, you may be a different species, but you are my whole world.

Lastly, to my readers (hopefully plural), thank you for bearing with me through the very weird ups and downs of this book, I really do hope you liked it.